Mountains

KINGFISHER

Published in 2012 by Kingfisher
This edition published in 2013 by Kingfisher
an imprint of Macmillan Children's Books
a division of Macmillan Publishers Limited
20 New Wharf Road, London N1 9RR
Basingstoke and Oxford
Associated companies throughout the world
www.panmacmillan.com

ISBN 978-0-7534-3724-7

First published as *Kingfisher Young Knowledge: Mountains* in 2007
Additional material produced for Macmillan Children's Books by Discovery Books Ltd

Copyright © Macmillan Children's Books 2012

1 3 5 7 9 8 6 4 2
1SPL/0713/WKT/UTD/128MA

A CIP catalogue record for this book is available from the British Library.

Printed in China

Note to readers: the website addresses listed in this book are correct at the time of going to print.
However, due to the ever-changing nature of the internet, website addresses and content can
change. Websites can contain links that are unsuitable for children. The publisher cannot be held
responsible for changes in website addresses or content, or for information obtained through
a third party. We strongly advise that internet searches be supervised by an adult.

Acknowledgements
The publisher would like to thank the following for permission to reproduce their material. Every care has been
taken to trace copyright holders. However, if there have been unintentional omissions or failure to trace copyright
holders, we apologise and will, if informed, endeavour to make corrections in any future edition.
b = bottom, c = centre, l = left, t = top, r = right

Photographs: *Cover* Shutterstock/Kuttelvaserova Stuchelova; *Pages* 1 Corbis/W Wayne Lockwood; 2–3 Corbis/Charlie Munsey;
4–5 Alamy/Nagelestock; 6–7 Corbis/Eye Ubiquitous; 7*tr* Corbis/Galen Rowell; 9 Shutterstock Images/fpolat;
10–11 Photolibrary.com; 11*br* Getty/Science Faction; 12 Corbis/Joseph Sohm; 13 Corbis/Ric Ergenbright; 15*tr* Frank Lane
Picture Agency/Winfried Wisniewski; 15*bl* Arboretum de Villardebelle, France; 16–17 Getty/Stone; 17*br* Alamy/Aflo Foto;
18*l* Corbis/Galen Rowell; 18–19 Getty/Imagebank; 19*r* Photolibrary.com; 20 Corbis/Eye Ubiquitous; 21*t* Corbis/Tom Bean;
21*br* Corbis/Paul A Souders; 22 Alamy/Brett Baunton; 23*t* Natural History Picture Agency/Alberto Nardi; 23*b* Science Photo
Library/Kaj R Svensson; 24 Corbis/Steve Kaufman; 25*t* Alamy/Imagina Photography; 25*b* Corbis/Joe McDonald; 26*c* Alamy/
Andrew Woodley; 26–27*b* Getty/Stone; 27*t* Alamy/Terry Fincher Photos; 28–29 Photolibrary.com; 29*t* Alamy/Mediacolor's;
30 Corbis/Zefa; 31*t* Getty/Photographer's Choice; 31*br* Getty/Aurora; 32 Getty/Digital Vision; 33*tl* Alamy/David R Frazier
Photolibrary; 33*b* Alamy/Phototake; 34 Alamy/Publiphoto Diffusion; 35*tl* John Cleare Mountain Camera; 35*b* Getty/
Photographer's Choice; 36*c* Royal Geographical Society; 36*br* Corbis Montagne Magazine; 37 Corbis/Sygma; 38 Alamy/
f1 online; 38–39 Alamy/StockShot; 39*c* Corbis/Ashley Cooper; 40 Corbis/EPA; 41*t* Corbis/John van Hasselt; 41*b* Frank Lane
Picture Agency/Foto Natura; 43*tl* Getty/NGS; 43*b* Mary Evans Picture Library; 48 Shutterstock Images/Ricardo Manuel Silva de
Sousa; 49*t* Shutterstock Images/steve100; 49*b* Shutterstock Images/Galyna Andrushko; 52 Shutterstock Images/Sam D Cruz;
53*bl* Shutterstock Images/Luigi Nifosi; 53*br* Shutterstock Images/Vulkanette; 56 Shutterstock Images/hipproductions

Illustrations on pages: 8, 11, 12, 13, 16 Peter Winfield; 14–15 Steve Weston

Commissioned photography on pages 44–47 by Andy Crawford
Thank you to models Jamie Chang-Leng, Mary Conquest and Georgina Page

Mountains

Margaret Hynes

KINGFISHER

Contents

What are mountains? **6**

Moving world **8**

Mountains of fire **10**

Rising rock **12**

On the mountainside **14**

Mountain weather **16**

Glaciers **18**

Wear and tear **20**

Plucky plants **22**

Adaptable animals **24**

Living on mountains **26**

Going places **28**

Tourism **30**

Mountain resources **32**

34 Mountaineering today

36 Reaching the top

38 Avalanche!

40 Mountain rescue

42 Mountain mysteries

44 Project: Making mountains

45 Project: Leaving footprints

46 Project: Moving cable car

48 Glossary

50 Parent and teacher notes

52 Did you know?

54 Mountains quiz

55 Find out more

56 Index

What are mountains?

A mountain is a giant, steep-sided rock that rises above the Earth's surface. There are mountains on land, under the oceans and even on other planets.

Mighty mountain ranges

A group of mountains is called a range. The Himalayas is a mountain range in Asia. It is home to the world's highest peaks.

Cold at the top

There is less, or thinner, air at the top of a mountain than there is at the bottom. It is also colder, so some peaks are snowy all year round.

Moving world

The Earth's rocky surface is called the crust. It is divided into plates, which fit together like a jigsaw. The plates move very slowly over the face of the Earth.

Moving plates

This map shows the plates and the direction they are moving in. Some plates crash into each other, while others pull apart.

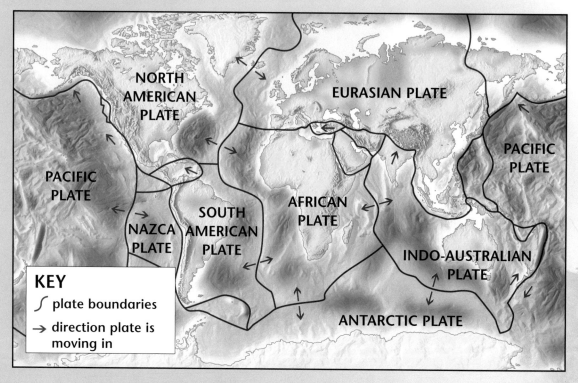

NORTH AMERICAN PLATE

EURASIAN PLATE

PACIFIC PLATE

PACIFIC PLATE

SOUTH AMERICAN PLATE

NAZCA PLATE

AFRICAN PLATE

INDO-AUSTRALIAN PLATE

ANTARCTIC PLATE

KEY

ʃ plate boundaries

→ direction plate is moving in

Earthquakes

When the edges of two plates
grip each other, the plates cannot
move. If they shift suddenly, an
earthquake happens, causing
terrible damage.

Mountains of fire

Some mountains are volcanoes. They form when hot, melted rock, called magma, erupts from a crack in the Earth's crust. The liquid rock cools and hardens into a mountain.

Violent eruption

Mount Etna is a volcano in Italy. When it erupts, magma bursts out. Ash, gas, steam and hot rocks shoot into the sky.

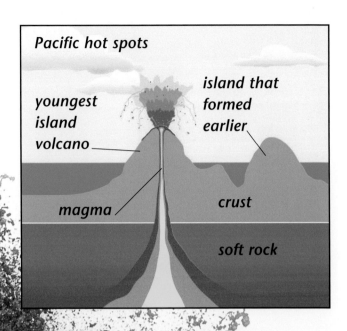

Pacific hot spots

youngest island volcano

island that formed earlier

magma

crust

soft rock

Hot spots

The Hawaiian islands are volcanoes. They form as the Pacific plate passes over a hot and active area under the Earth's crust called a hot spot.

Flowing lava

Once magma pours out of a volcano, it is called lava. It rolls downhill, like a river of fire.

Rising rock

Many mountains form in areas where plates push against each other. The moving plates squeeze the land up, creating mountains.

squeezing action pushes up blocks of rock

Fault-block mountains

The moving plates can cause cracks in the crust. These break the crust into blocks and some rise up to form fault-block mountains.

plate A *plate B*

Rounded off

The Wasatch range in Utah, USA, is a fault-block mountain range. Its blocky shape has been worn down over time.

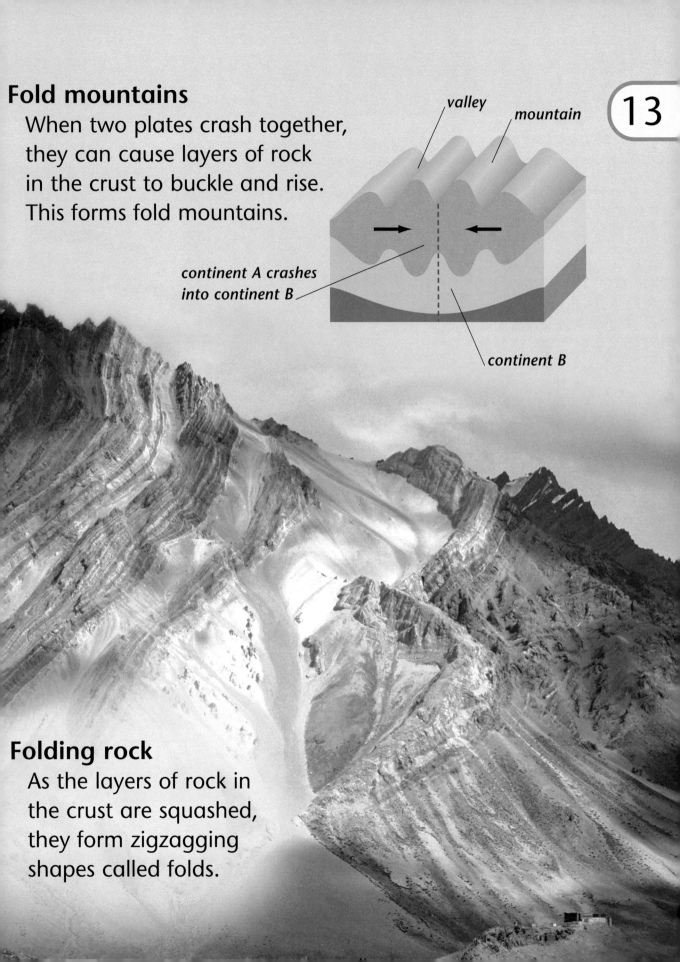

Fold mountains

When two plates crash together, they can cause layers of rock in the crust to buckle and rise. This forms fold mountains.

valley

mountain

continent A crashes into continent B

continent B

Folding rock

As the layers of rock in the crust are squashed, they form zigzagging shapes called folds.

On the mountainside

A high mountain has several zones, or regions. Each zone has different plants and animals. Very few plants or animals live near the top.

Plant cover

Forests cover the mountain's lower region. Further up is a zone of small, low-lying plants called alpines.

conifers

deciduous trees

icy peak

alpine region

Mountain birds

The wind is so strong at the top of mountains that only powerful birds, such as this lammergeier, can fly there.

Conifers

These cones and pine needles belong to the spruce conifer. Conifer trees have a triangular shape. This helps the snow to slide off them.

Mountain weather

The weather can change very quickly on mountains. A storm can start in just a few minutes. The temperature can quickly drop to below freezing.

Rain shelter

Some mountains are so high they block rain clouds. One slope may be rainy while the other side stays dry.

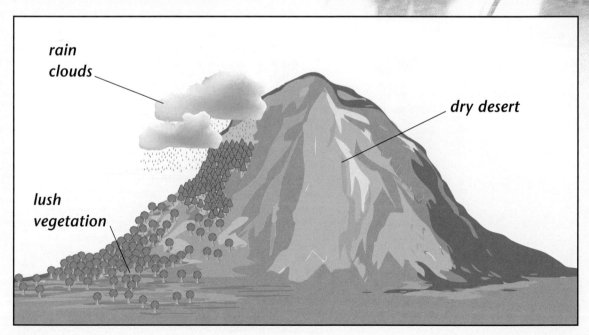

rain clouds

dry desert

lush vegetation

Blizzards

Howling winds whip up mountain snow into storms called blizzards. These make climbing much more difficult.

Burning Sun

Sunlight passes through the thin mountain air easily. Snow reflects the rays of light on to skin, and this can cause sunburn, even in the cold.

Glaciers

Great rivers of ice, called glaciers, form on the peaks of some of the world's highest mountains. The glaciers move downhill very slowly.

How glaciers form

Snow collects in rocky hollows, called cirques, high up the mountain. The snow turns into ice, and forms a glacier.

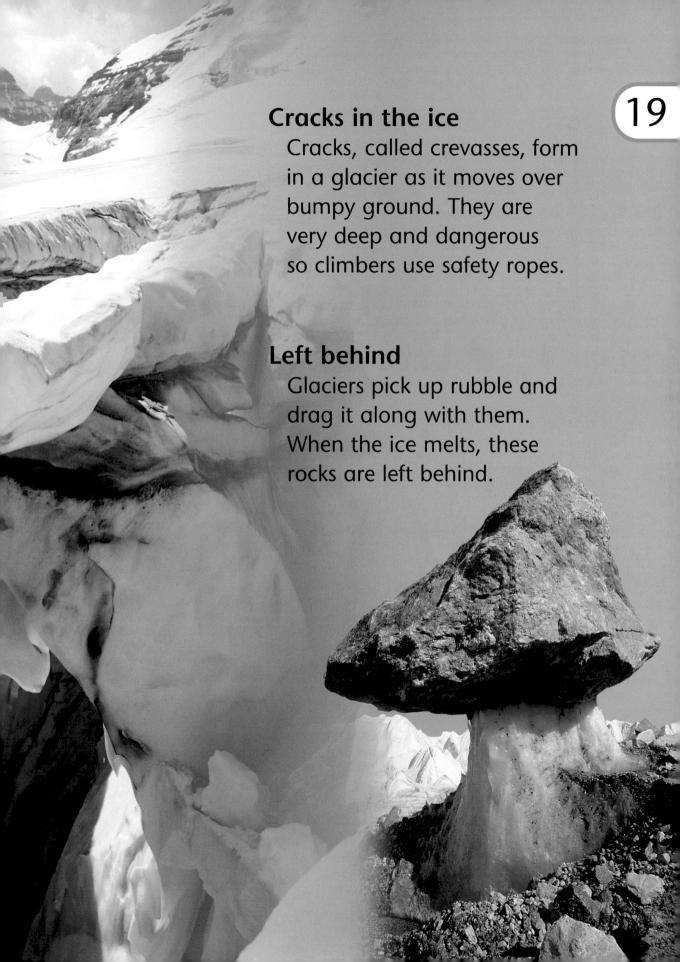

Cracks in the ice

Cracks, called crevasses, form in a glacier as it moves over bumpy ground. They are very deep and dangerous so climbers use safety ropes.

Left behind

Glaciers pick up rubble and drag it along with them. When the ice melts, these rocks are left behind.

Wear and tear

All mountains are under attack from the elements. Ice, wind and running water slowly wear them down over millions of years.

Old mountain

A young mountain is jagged. As it gets older, the elements slowly wear it down and it becomes more rounded.

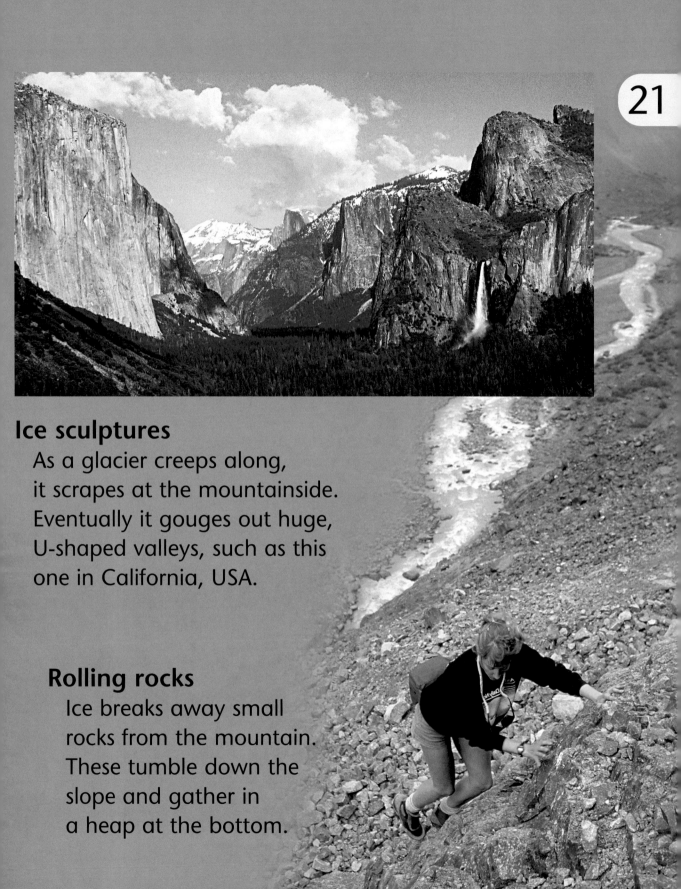

Ice sculptures

As a glacier creeps along,
it scrapes at the mountainside.
Eventually it gouges out huge,
U-shaped valleys, such as this
one in California, USA.

Rolling rocks

Ice breaks away small
rocks from the mountain.
These tumble down the
slope and gather in
a heap at the bottom.

Plucky plants

Plants that grow high up on the mountain slopes have adapted to cope with the biting cold, fierce winds and freezing weather there.

Tiny trees

Some willow and birch trees grow high up the mountainside. They avoid the howling winds by hugging the ground.

Alpine snowbell

The alpine snowbell gives off heat, which melts the snow around it. The plant's heat enables it to bloom in spring.

Growing on rocks

Lichens live on rocky peaks. They make acids that make the rocks crumble. Then they send tiny roots into the rocks to suck up any goodness in them.

Adaptable animals

Some animals that live on mountains have adapted to cope with the steep slopes. Others have adapted to living with high winds and freezing conditions.

Hot bath

Japanese macaque monkeys wallow in hot pools during the cold winters. The water is heated by volcanoes.

Mountain climber

Mountain goats are good at scrabbling over the rocky mountain faces. Their hooves are hollow and act like suction pads, helping the goats to grip.

Natural anti-freeze

The Yarrow's spiny lizard's blood stays liquid in temperatures below freezing, so it can survive on icy peaks in Mexico.

Living on mountains

Mountain peoples have learned to live in steep, remote and sometimes dangerous places. They grow crops for food and raise animals there.

Mountain animals

Yaks are useful animals. They provide farmers with food and wool. They are also used to carry goods.

Mountain cities

Kathmandu nestles in the Himalayas. It has the same facilities as any other modern city.

Growing food

Mountain fields are steep and there is not much soil. Many farmers build terraces to stop the soil washing away.

Going places

It can be difficult to travel on mountains because they are very steep. People have come up with clever ways for making mountain travel easier.

Long and winding roads

Mountain roads do not follow a straight line because they would be too steep to climb. The roads take a zigzagging route instead.

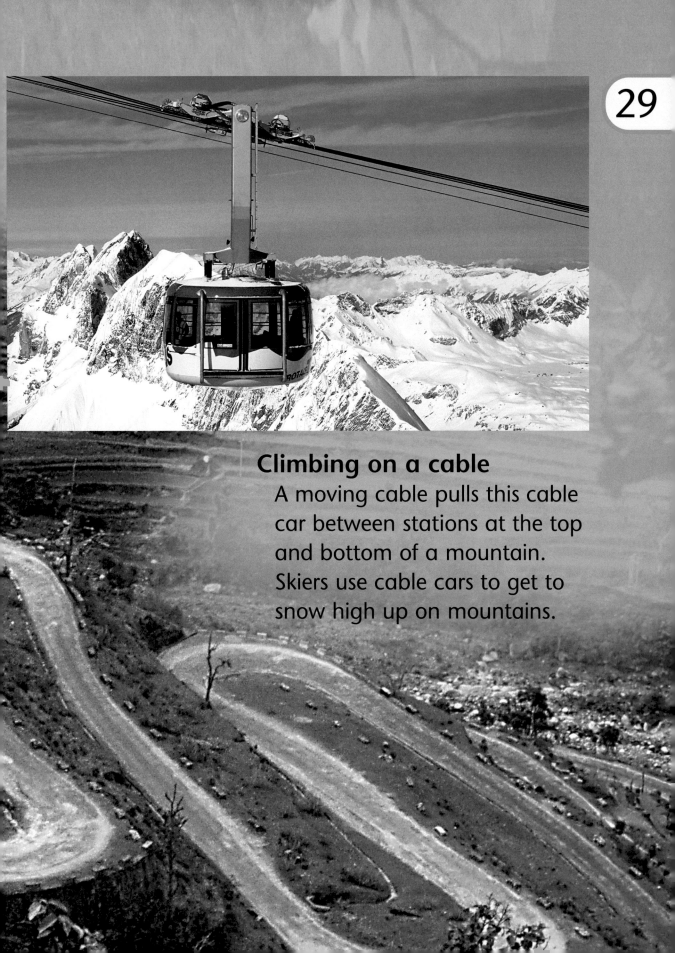

Climbing on a cable

A moving cable pulls this cable car between stations at the top and bottom of a mountain. Skiers use cable cars to get to snow high up on mountains.

Tourism

Mountains are great places to explore and enjoy. People can ski, trek, climb or mountain bike along the steep slopes. But we must protect these places so that everyone can enjoy them in the future.

Jumping off

Hang-gliders jump off mountain tops to float down on their wings. They glide on the warm air that rises from the ground.

Winter sports

Skiers and snowboarders
love snow-covered
mountains. They can
slide and jump down
the slippery slopes.

Mountain of rubbish

Many tourists drop their
rubbish on mountain
visits. This pollutes the
area and can harm the
wildlife that lives there.

Mountain resources

Hidden inside mountains lie valuable resources, such as building materials and metals. There are also useful resources on the slopes, such as trees.

Building blocks

Each day, big dumper trucks remove tonnes of rock and rubble from mountains. It is used to make buildings and bridges.

Cutting down trees

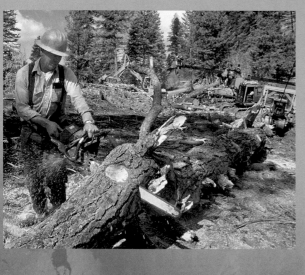

Logging companies plant fast-growing trees on mountainsides. When the trees are grown, loggers cut them down for timber and fuel.

Mining metal

Some mountain rocks are rich in gold, silver, copper and tin. Miners use large drills to dig these metals out of the stone.

Mountaineering today

Today's mountaineers are well prepared for their climbs. They have special food for energy, layers of clothing for warmth and lots of safety equipment.

A good night's rest
Mountaineers shelter in tents at night and in bad weather. The tents are light to carry, strong and waterproof.

Oxygen supply

Climbers carry tanks of oxygen, which they use to help them to breathe more easily in the thin mountain air.

Climbing suit

Climbers wear one-piece suits filled with down for warmth. The suit is windproof and waterproof.

Reaching the top

Mountain climbing is a popular sport. Many people have now climbed even the highest mountains, including the tallest on land, Mount Everest.

George Mallory

Andrew Irvine

Last climb

Mallory and Irvine began to climb Everest in 1924. Both men died on the mountain, but no one knows if they reached the top before they died.

Extraordinary climber

Reinhold Messner has climbed the world's 14 highest peaks. He was the first person to climb Everest without extra oxygen.

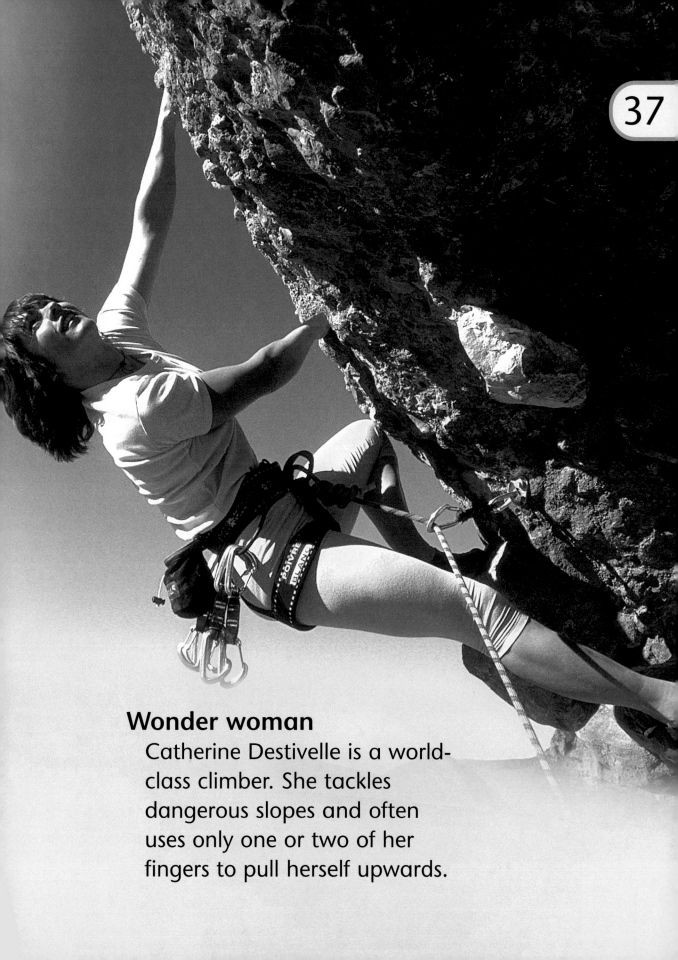

Wonder woman

Catherine Destivelle is a world-
class climber. She tackles
dangerous slopes and often
uses only one or two of her
fingers to pull herself upwards.

Avalanche!

A large mass of snow and ice can suddenly break loose and crash down a mountainside. This is called an avalanche.

Predicting avalanches

Scientists use information gathered in weather stations like this one to help them predict when avalanches are likely.

Avalanche in action

Some avalanches move as fast as a racing car. They sweep away everything in their path, including trees, people and even villages.

Protection

This steel fence has been built to stop an avalanche from reaching the town further downhill. It will slow down an avalanche.

Mountain **rescue**

Even experienced mountaineers can get into trouble on mountains. When they do, well-equipped and specially trained teams are ready to race to the rescue.

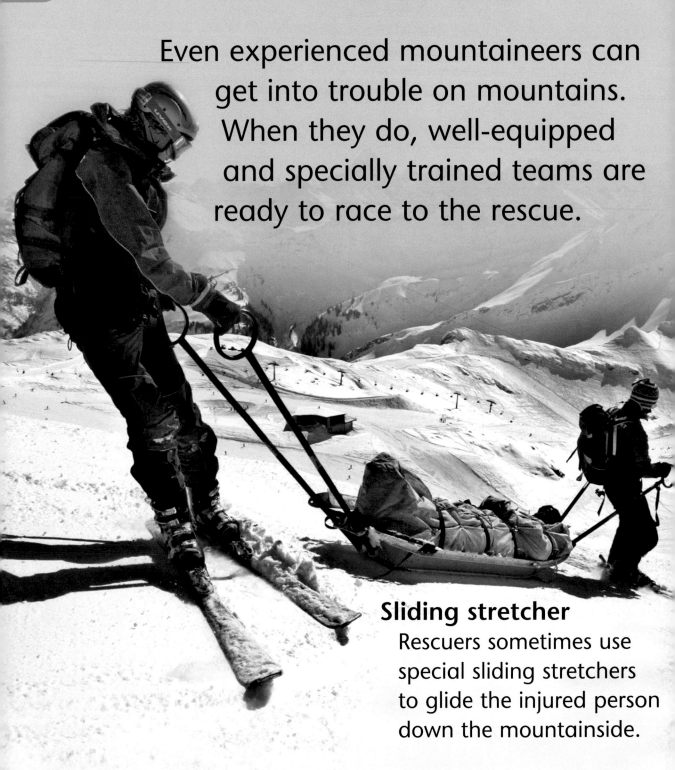

Sliding stretcher
Rescuers sometimes use special sliding stretchers to glide the injured person down the mountainside.

Helicopter rescue

Helicopters can reach remote peaks quickly. Rescuers can then help the injured people and take them to hospital.

Rescue dog

St Bernard dogs have a strong sense of smell. They can be specially trained to sniff out the victims of avalanches.

Mountain mysteries

People sometimes see some strange things when they climb a mountain. They might find fossil fish, or they might be followed by a huge shadow.

Ghostly shadow

If someone climbs a mountain when the Sun is low, the Sun casts an enormous shadow on any low clouds.

Something fishy

People often find fossil fish in rocks in fold mountains. Millions of years ago, these mountains were part of the seafloor.

Bigfoot

Some people believe a large creature called Bigfoot roams the Rocky Mountains in North America. No one knows if it really exists.

Making mountains

Make a fold mountain range

Discover how land is forced upwards when two plates collide by doing this simple experiment.

Roll out each ball of clay to make a rough square 25mm thick.

You will need
- 2 balls of modelling clay, different colours
- Tray
- Rolling pin
- Plastic food wrap

Lay both pieces 10mm apart on the plastic food wrap on the tray.

Gently push the two clay blocks together. Your mountain range will rise upwards.

Leaving footprints

Bigfoot's calling card

Bigfoot's footprints are called its 'calling card'. Make one to give to a friend.

You will need
- Large sheet of card
- Paints and paintbrush
- Marker pen or felt-tip pen
- Scissors
- Sponge

1 Fold the card in half, then paint a big foot shape. Cut out the shape, but do not cut the folded side.

2 On a sponge, draw a smaller foot shape. Cut this out.

3 Dip the sponge in some paint and decorate your card with lots of little footprints walking up towards the toes.

Your giant calling card is ready. Write a message inside.

Moving cable car

Make a cable car
Cable cars can climb high mountains on moving cables. Make a model with stations at the top and bottom of your mountain range.

You will need
- 3 small cereal boxes
- Coloured paper
- Sharp pencil
- Modelling clay
- 1 long, 1 short piece of string
- Marbles
- Sticky tape
- 1 small sweet box

1 Cover the cereal boxes with coloured paper. Decorate with shapes of mountains and trees.

2 Pierce a hole in the top of each box with a sharp pencil. Use modelling clay to push against.

3 Thread the long piece of string through the holes as shown.

4 Place some marbles in each box, then tape the boxes shut.

5

Decorate the small sweet box with coloured paper to make it look like a cable car.

6

Tape the short piece of string to the car, then tie it to the middle of the long piece of string.

Place the top station on a box. By pulling on the long piece of string, you can move your cable car from the station at the bottom, up the mountain to the station at the top.

Acids – substances that can eat away other substances

Adapted – changed over time

Air – the mixture of gases that we breathe

Buckle – to crumple and fold

Cable – a long, thick rope usually made from metal wire

Conifer – an evergreen tree that keeps its leaves all year round

Crust – the hard, rocky surface of the Earth

Deciduous tree – a tree that loses its leaves in autumn

Down – soft, hair-like feathers that cover young birds

Earthquake – shaking of the ground caused by a sudden movement in the Earth's crust

Elements – strong winds, heavy rain and other kinds of bad weather

Erupt – to explode, throwing ash, gas and hot rocks into the air

Experienced – describes people who have skill which they have gained over time

Facilities – buildings and services, such as health care and schools

Fossil – the remains of ancient animals or plants found in rock

Fuel – a substance burnt to produce heat or power

Glide – to move smoothly and quietly

Gouge – to make a hole in something with force

Hollow – a shallow hole

Jagged – describes a surface that is sharp and uneven

Lichen – a slow-growing plant that forms crusty branches on rocks, walls and trees

Oxygen – a common gas in the air that is necessary for human life

Peak – the top part of a mountain

Plates – large areas of land that 'float' on the liquid rock underneath

Pollute – to make harmful waste that damages the environment

Predict – to say what will happen in the future

Ray – a beam of light that travels in a straight line

Reflect – to bounce back from a surface

Remote – describes out-of-the-way places

Resources – raw materials that can be used to make other things

Rubble – a mixture of stones and rocks of different sizes

Seafloor – the land at the bottom of the sea

Steel – a strong metal made from iron and carbon

Suction – the process that occurs when two surfaces stick together because the air between them has been removed

Terraces – fields with steps going down a hillside

Vegetation – plant life

World-class – among the best in the world

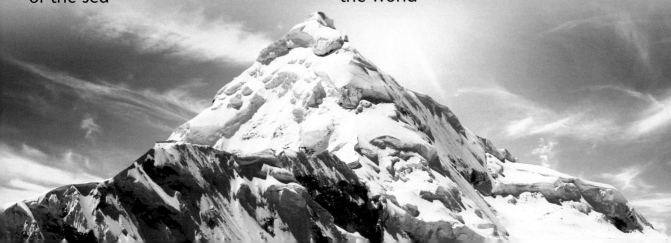

This book includes material that would be particularly useful in helping to teach children aged 7–11. It covers many elements of the English and Science curricula and provides opportunities for cross-curricular lessons, especially those involving Geography and Art.

Extension activities

Writing
Read about Mallory and Irvine on page 36. Imagine what happened to them as they climbed Everest, and write it as a set of diary entries. Say if you think they reached the top or not before they died.

Read about the ghostly shadows on page 42, and write a poem describing your shadow as you climb a mountain.

Speaking and listening
Imagine you are reporter witnessing a volcanic eruption. Describe what you see.

Science
Background information is provided on the scientific themes of rocks (pp19, 20–21, 32–33), Earth (pp6–7, 8–9, 10–11, 12–13), habitats (pp14–15, 22–23, 24–25, 26–27) and forces (pp29, 30–31, 38–39, 40).

Find some different types of rock near where you live. Compare them: do they look or feel different? Do they float or sink? Do they soak up water? Are they hard or soft? How heavy are they? Can you see grains in them? Are any magnetic? Display your findings in a chart.

How is the air different higher up a mountain? Write a short report describing how this affects people. Pages 7, 17 and 35 will help you with your research.

Read pages 10–11. Make your own volcano by putting some baking soda (sodium bicarbonate) into a container and pouring in vinegar (acetic acid), then watch the eruption. Use your craft skills to make the volcano look even more realistic.

Cross-curricular links

Geography: Find ten mountain ranges in an atlas, and make a list showing which countries they are in. Try to find out the name of the highest mountain in each range as well.

What is the nearest mountain to where you live? Is it young or old? How do you think it was formed? Use pages 20–21 to help you.

Art: Look at the picture on page 16. Make a collage of a mountain scene where only one side is rainy. Can you make your collage 3-D?

Art/design/geography: Can you make a terraced mountain? You will need to cut the outline of a mountain as seen from above onto cardboard. Then cut slightly smaller outlines and glue each layer on top. You will slowly build a terraced mountain.

Using the projects

Children can follow or adapt these projects at home. Here are some ideas for extending them:

Page 44: Form the modelling clay into two cylinder shapes and push them together. What happens if you pull them apart at the ends?

Page 45: Make a footprint in a tray of soil or sand. Pour plaster mixed with water into it so it is covered. When the plaster is set, lift up your 'fossilized' footprint.

Page 46–47: Can you create a mountain landscape for your cable car?

Did you know?

- Some mountain ranges are older than others. The Highlands in Scotland are 400 million years old, while the Alps in central Europe are only 15 million years old.

- The longest mountain range in the world is the Andes in South America. The mountains stretch for over 7,000 kilometres.

- The slam of a car door, a falling branch or the movement of a skier can all start an avalanche. Snow can speed down a mountain at 320 kilometres per hour!

- Glaciers store about 70 per cent of the world's supply of fresh water and cover about 10 per cent of the Earth's land.

- At the top of the Himalayas, fierce winds can reach more than 300 kilometres per hour.

- The highest altitude at which trees will grow is called the tree line. The highest tree line in the world is in the Bolivian Andes, where hardy trees can grow up to 5,200 metres above sea level.

- K2 is the second highest mountain on Earth after Everest. It is known as the 'Savage Mountain'. One in five people that have tried to reach the top have died. Only 302 people have ever made it to the summit, compared to the 2,700 that have scaled Everest. K2 has never been climbed in winter.

- Measured from the base, the tallest mountain is not Everest but Hawaii's Mauna Kea, which rises to a height of 9,500 metres from the seafloor.

- Because the temperature at the top of a mountain is much colder than at the bottom, it is possible to have snow at the equator, the warmest part of the world.

- The Himalayan jumping spider lives higher up than any other animal. At around 6,700 metres, its only food is insects blown by the wind from lower levels.

- The plates that folded up to form the Himalayas are still crashing into each other. Some mountains, such as Everest, continue to grow higher by about a centimetre each year!

- Mount Stromboli, on a small Italian island, is one of the world's most active volcanoes. It has been erupting almost non-stop for the past 20,000 years!

- Mountain people and animals can live at great heights because they have bigger hearts and lungs, which carry more blood and oxygen.

- The world's highest ever cable car system was located in the city of Mérida in Venezuela. It was over 12 kilometres long and reached a height of nearly 4,800 metres.

- Tourism brings a lot of money for the people who live in the mountains. The Alps receives about 100 million visitors every year.

Mountains quiz

The answers to these questions can all be found by looking back through the book. See how many you get right. You can check your answers on page 56.

1) Which mountain range is home to the world's highest peaks?
   A – Andes
   B – Himalayas
   C – Alps

2) When do mountains form?
   A – When two plates push against each other
   B – When two plates stay still
   C – When two plates move away from each other

3) Where is air the thinnest in the mountains?
   A – Down in the valleys
   B – At the tops
   C – Among the pine trees

4) What is a large crack in a glacier called?
   A – Lammergeier
   B – Crevasse
   C – Cirque

5) Which of these does not make rocks crumble?
   A – Sunlight
   B – Lichens
   C – Glaciers

6) Why do farmers build terraces?
   A – To separate different crops
   B – To attract tourists
   C – To stop the soil washing away

7) Which of these is used to get up a mountain?
   A – Cable car
   B – Hang-glider
   C – Snowboard

8) What valuable material can be found in mountains?
   A – Glass
   B – Plastic
   C – Metal

9) Reinhold Messner was the first person to climb Everest without…
   A – A tent
   B – Extra oxygen
   C – Food

10) What breed of dog is used to sniff out the victims of avalanches?
    A – Jack Russell
    B – St Bernard
    C – Pug

11) Which can move downhill the quickest?
    A – A glacier
    B – An avalanche
    C – A skier

12) Where is Bigfoot believed to live?
    A – Kathmandu
    B – Hawaiian islands
    C – Rocky Mountains

Find out more

Books to read

Earth's Shifting Surface (Sci-Hi) by Robert Snedden, Heinemann Library, 2010

I Wonder Why Mountains Have Snow On Top by Jackie Gaff, Kingfisher, 2012

Life Cycles: Mountain by Sean Callery, Kingfisher, 2012

The Mountain Environment (Step-up Geography) by Clare Hibbert, Evans Brothers, 2005

Mountain Food Chains (Protecting Food Chains) by Rachel Lynette, Heinemann Library, 2011

Mountains (Extreme Habitats) by Susie Hodge, TickTock Books, 2007

Mountains (Go Facts: Natural Environments) by Ian Rohr, A&C Black, 2009

Places to visit

Nevis Range, near Fort William, Scotland
www.nevisrange.co.uk
Learn about the wildlife, habitats and landscape that surround Ben Nevis, the highest mountain in the UK. Depending on the season, the resort offers a range of activities, from walking and mountain biking to skiing and snowboarding. You can also enjoy a cable car ride up the mountain to a height of 650 metres.

Snowdon Mountain Railway, North Wales
www.snowdonrailway.co.uk
Take a railway trip to the very top of Snowdon, the highest mountain in Wales. The visitor centre at the top is the highest building in England and Wales.

Highland Wildlife Park, Kincraig, Scotland
www.highlandwildlifepark.org
Discover some of the creatures that live in mountain habitats around the world in this spectacular wildlife park. Highlights include red pandas, Przewalski horses and Japanese macaques.

Websites

http://vulcan.wr.usgs.gov/Outreach/AboutVolcanoes/framework.html
Why do volcanoes occur? When will a volcano erupt? How hot is a volcano? Find out the answers to these and other questions on this site.

http://primaryhomeworkhelp.co.uk/mountains/types.htm
On this site for primary school children find out how different types of mountains are formed.

www.onegeology.org/eXtra/kids/earthProcesses/glaciers.html
This website lets you explore Earth's processes. You can find out all about glaciers, including how they form, how they move and how they melt.

air 7, 17, 35
animals 24–25, 26, 53
avalanches 52, 38–39, 41
Bigfoot 43, 45
birds 15
building materials 32
cable cars 29, 46–47, 53
climbing 34–35, 36–37, 52
crust 8, 9
earthquakes 9
farmers 26, 27
fault-block mountains 12
fold mountains 13, 44
footprints 45
fossils 43
glaciers 18–19, 21, 52
ice 18–19, 20, 21, 38
lava 11
magma 10, 11

mining 33
mountaineering 34–35, 36–37
mountain rescue 40–41
mysteries 42–43
peaks 6, 7, 36
people 26–27, 53
plants 14–15, 22–23
plates 8–9, 11, 12–13, 53
rain 16
resources 32–33
roads 28
snow 7, 17, 18, 23, 31, 38–39, 52
storms 15, 17
tourism 30–31, 53
travel 28–29
trees 14–15, 22, 33, 52
volcanoes 10–11, 24, 53
weather 16–17, 22, 38
winds 15, 17, 20, 22, 24, 52, 53

Mountains quiz answers	
1) B	7) A
2) A	8) C
3) B	9) B
4) B	10) B
5) A	11) B
6) C	12) C